Every Employee's Guide to Customer Satisfaction

How To Make Customers Return & Recommend

By Bart Allen Berry

Copyright © 2018 Bart Allen Berry
Paperback Edition

ISBN: 9781728967752

Written by Bart Allen Berry

All rights reserved. No part of this publication may be reproduced, distributed or transmitted in any form or by any means, or stored in a database or retrieval system, without the prior written permission of the publisher.

Please contact us for video or audio course information about this title.
www.BartBerry.com

"Getting your customers to return to and recommend your business is one of the most important factors to the success of any business.

By understanding the research-based statistical predictors of satisfaction (The Values of Excellence) this book will help guide every employee to do the things that get customers to come back and to recommend the business to others

– for any industry, for any product or service.

-Bart Allen Berry

Bart Allen Berry is a veteran organizational development consultant, researcher, trainer, author and speaker. Bart has worked with hundreds of companies over the past 32 years and delivered training to more than 200,000 employees and managers worldwide.

See Bart's other books, articles and organizational assessments at: http://www.BartBerry.com

Table of Contents

Introduction   3

I.   **Customer Satisfaction – The Big Picture**   6

II.   **How to Be Excellent**   22

III.   **Employee Self Assessment**   50

IV.   **Listening to Your Customers**   60

Appendix: 69
Forty Four Employee Tips To Improve Customer Satisfaction

Introduction

First of all, what we're talking about when we say Customer Satisfaction is the 'end state' your customers are in when they walk out the door or end a transaction with you - whether you provide a product or a service or specific work for an employer. Customer Satisfaction is a measurement of how satisfied they are with *'The Complete Customer Experience'*. Customer Satisfaction should not be confused with 'Customer Service' – which is included as a sub-set of the actions and behaviors that you take to help create the end state called Customer Satisfaction.

What you will learn in this course is that Customer Service is covered in just one of what I call The Ten Values of Excellence that are present in any transaction with customers, or in the delivery of any product or service. These ten values, according to our research with over 2 million customers, **are *the ten factors that most strongly influence how satisfied customers will be*,** and ultimately – whether they will return to buy again or recommend you or your business to others. You're going to learn about each of these in this book.

Any of the Ten Values of Excellence can be made stronger or neglected entirely by you the employee – thus having a positive or negative impact on The Complete Customer Experience.

While most of these factors are within your control when dealing with customers – especially the human factors, there are potentially process factors and structural factors (perhaps policy and procedure guidelines of your employer) that will be outside of your ability to impact – thus making the things you *can* have a direct impact on more critical to happy, healthy and satisfied customer relationships.

This course is all about how you can apply these values in all of your customer-supplier relationships and how you can positively influence customers – and directly affect the strength and success of any business. Since most employers want you to represent them well with customers, and they want these customers to return to buy again and to recommend the business to others- you will be making yourself more valuable to the business if you can become instrumental in creating more satisfied customers. Every business is on a customer satisfaction improvement journey.

Whatever your level or position in your business or company, the Ten Values of Excellence will always be applicable because they are the research based validated factors *that customers say they are looking for*, what makes them satisfied and what makes them come back. They can be applied to any enterprise, at every level and they never go out of style.

As a customer yourself you will resonate with everything in this course, and for the first time have a methodical system of understanding about how customer satisfaction is created, and how it can be destroyed. This information will serve you for your entire professional career.

I. Customer Satisfaction – The Big Picture

In the past Customer Satisfaction was not well understood and generally referred mainly to customer service practices (as previously mentioned). Through significant research with mountains of customer data we have learned how to better define, measure and predict what customer satisfaction is, how, when and why it happens.

Let's remember that Customer Satisfaction is *an effect* – or end state based upon the complete customer experience – that means everything that happens to the customer when they deal with you, your product or service delivery. There are many more factors at play – in a restaurant for example – than the quality of the hamburger. The entire customer experience might include a dirty or clean restaurant environment, courteous or rude wait staff, a hard to find location or one that closes too early, arcane ordering processes, slow service or one of many other reasons.

The point here is that any of these factors and more as we will be discussing, can cause the customer to leave the restaurant in one of three distinct states:

DISSATISFIED INDIFFERENT OR SATISFIED and the degree to which they have experienced one these states will determine how they will behave when it comes to return and recommend behavior.

Let's look at the diagram below:

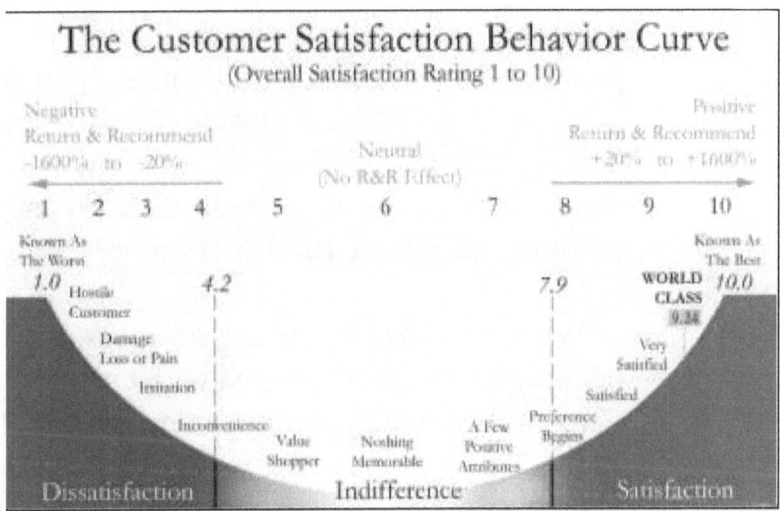

DISSATISFACTION

As we see in this diagram called 'The Customer Satisfaction Behavior Curve', we use a 1 to 10 scale to measure overall satisfaction. Notice that there are the three distinct zones we are talking about. If a customer rated their overall customer experience as a 4.1 or lower that falls into the zone of customer dissatisfaction. The important thing to understand here is that this is the zone where customers not only don't return to the business, but they begin to say negative things – and they tell more people, the more dissatisfied they are.

This is bad news for the business because this is where a bad reputation is formed and depending upon the severity of the dissatisfaction, these people will be telling lots of people, who will also be telling lots of people who will tell lots of people... you get the idea. In terms of percentages, if customers are consistently rating a business this low that means they can have a negative return and recommend rate of 1000% or higher!

Wow, this means that the business can become known as the worst with customers who go from being inconvenienced, to irritated, to real damage, loss or pain, to outright hostility from customers. This is where lawsuits can happen and businesses can be closed.

Now since all of the Ten Values of Excellence can play a role in effecting the customer experience, it is important to score high enough in each one so that customers don't rate you in the zone of customer dissatisfaction. (More about these values later).

INDIFFERENCE
The next Zone in rating the customer experience is called the Zone of Customer

Indifference from 4.2 to 7.8. Like it sounds, customers are not too excited about a business with satisfaction scores in this zone. We often see these types of scores in mediocre businesses that might have one or two positive attributes, dramatic sales or specials that attract customers, or perhaps a convenient location that makes them the only choice in the area. Indifference is important to understand because while the business is not necessarily in danger of closing with these scores, it is not thriving either. Customers who deal with this supplier are not loyal customers who are necessarily returning or recommending the business to others. Customer Return and Recommend scores in this zone are 0%!

Humans love to talk about the exciting and memorable things that happen in their lives – either negative or positive, but they rarely share the stories of their mediocre experiences. That's what's happening here. But at least, they aren't saying anything bad.

SATISFACTION
The Zone of Satisfaction in our model here ranges from an overall customer experience score of 7.9 to 10.0. This is actually a fairly high range and later we'll be introducing an audit process where you'll be able to measure overall satisfaction yourself so you can

understand how we get these scores. In the SATISFACTION range, 20% of customers begin returning to the business or recommending it to others all the way to 1600% of customers! How can we have more than 100% of customers returning or recommending? That's because this is the formation of a positive reputation – people who have never even been to the business themselves have heard great things about it and are telling others. As scores get higher and higher customers go from satisfied to very satisfied and even higher to the point where they might be calling a business 'world class' or 'known as the best'. Think of the successful brands you know who have achieved this type of reputation. Examples might include Rolex, Mercedes Benz, Luis Vuitton, Apple, Gucci, Nordstroms etc.

   Businesses with customer satisfaction scores this high are serious competitors and will generally dominate their geographic area – like a great restaurant that gets all the business, or might be successful enough to dominate their industry and will be recognized as 'best practice' or what we call 'the benchmark' – meaning that they are the one to be compared to.
   Businesses (or suppliers) with very high customer satisfaction scores won't have to

spend as much money on advertising or work as hard to get new customers because they are already getting so much free advertising from positive word of mouth. A struggling business with lower scores might have to spend a lot more money on advertising and promotions etc. to acquire new customers – and then if they don't satisfy them adequately – won't even get the benefit of having the customer return. That's an expensive way to run a business.

THE CUSTOMER SUPPLIER RELATIONSHIP

The Customer-Supplier Relationship is at the heart of where customer satisfaction is created.

The terms customer and supplier are used throughout this course to describe the roles of the 'Supplier'- the one providing the product, service, benefit etc. (with you representing them as an employee) and the 'Customer', the one buying or receiving the product or service. Healthcare provider and patient, mechanic and car owner, government employee and citizen tax payer, server and restaurant customer, software designer and computer user – you get the idea.

The relationship between these roles is a dynamic one, but it is worth examining to see how the Values of Excellence are integrated to enhance this relationship to create success and satisfaction,

Or

Where they are lacking - creating a relationship breakdown.

The customer-supplier relationship contains an assumed contract between the parties.

The customer wants or needs to get something from the supplier, and the supplier wants or needs to give something to the customer. The degree to which the supplier demonstrates The Ten Values of Excellence will determine the level of satisfaction in the customer experience and whether or not the relationship will continue and repeat over time, and whether the customer will recommend the supplier to other potential customers.

The Ten Values of Excellence are the framework for customer-supplier relationship excellence.

Customers want to have a relationship.

Few suppliers start out with an understanding of this basic assumption. Customers expect the supplier to welcome their business and to be prepared and geared-up for serving their needs. From the beginning, they expect the supplier to want to discuss their needs and to take an interest in their situation.

The supplier needs to understand that this relationship starts out with a positive expectation from the customer. You, representing the supplier in this relationship are always in the position to demonstrate your willingness to participate in a win-win relationship, but without appropriate attention to the customer, may drop the ball before a relationship can ever begin.

To be effective, supplier's need to be proactive about establishing and maintaining a relationship with their customers-- over as long a period of time as possible.

The Excellence Value of 'Connection' (being open and available, convenient and easy to connect with), Environment (having a clean and safe warm and welcoming place of business), and Self-Management (courteous and attentive pleasant front-line customer service) will help communicate openness and receptivity from the first positive interaction with a new customer that immediately starts the relationship off on the right foot.

Even when customers are doing digital business with an automated website, the design of the experience can still communicate excellence so a positive digital relationship ca be created and supported.

The first interaction is of critical importance to the establishment of the kind of relationship the customer wants to have. Our research shows that customers want and expect to have a positive relationship with the supplier – it is up to you to make this happen. Keep this in mind with every customer you meet.

The importance of the win-win relationship.

In a win-win relationship, both parties' benefit. This should be the actual target and goal of the supplier. Rather than just maximizing profit with a customer once, the supplier is potentially setting up the basis for ongoing sales - or in the case of a customer only buying once - a reputation for a quality experience that this customer will share with others.

In a Win-Win relationship the customer gets their needs met with a high level of quality, value, efficiency, courtesy etc. and the supplier gets compensated with a contract, wages, or other reward. Win-win relationships tend to repeat themselves, **and are the only type of relationships that are sustainable over time.**

Fundamentally, the supplier (and you the employee) should be continually evaluating the way they are relating to their customers- would this feel like Win-Win to me? Consciously or unconsciously your customer will conclude their transaction with a good feeling, confidence in the Supplier, an impression of excellence or regretfully, something else. As a supplier do you start out with the idea of a win-win relationship?

Every advertisement, retail sign, TV commercial, internet banner ad, or product label is an invitation to "Come and have a relationship-- we will provide what you want or need". The premise is always that this will be a win-win relationship. If you vote for me I will do this for you, if you buy this car you will get quality, value, dependability, etc.

In an ideal world, every transaction would result in suppliers totally fulfilling their promises and meeting or exceeding customer expectations. If this really happened we would only need one supplier in every industry. Suppliers that create real excellence in the eyes of customers like this -and establish totally satisfied brand loyalty is in reality, quite rare.

Win-win relationships are reflected in the 'Zone of Satisfaction' on the Customer Satisfaction Behavior Curve (7.9 or higher) and are characterized by customers who return to buy again, and provide referrals and unsolicited testimonials with increasing intensity as their satisfaction increases.

A World Class Excellent Supplier (9.24 or higher) enjoys close to a 1600% return and recommend rate because their satisfied customers are telling everyone, and those folks are telling others, who are telling others because the product, service, management, leadership, talent, work etc. is excellent! These free advertisements are normal for World Class Suppliers - known as unsolicited testimonials.

Customers who rate the supplier as World Class really feel like they are winning in the relationship. When levels of satisfaction are not achieved, return and recommend slips, and the relationship begins to deteriorate from preference or a feeling of win-win to indifference, and eventually dissatisfaction (Win -lose). Our satisfaction studies always use a rating scale of 1 (lowest) to 10 (highest) because we can see the subtle changes in customer satisfaction and behavior as ratings slide or grow.

The deteriorating relationship.

The customer satisfaction behavior curve clearly illustrates the rapid fall off of customer loyalty that happens as customers become less satisfied and when suppliers are perceived as less than excellent.

A deteriorating relationship means vulnerability for the supplier.

When they aren't satisfied, voters look for alternate candidates, local restaurant patrons consider trying a different eatery, long time Chevrolet loyalists start looking at Volkswagens, or employers start paying closer attention to the new resumes that come across their desk.

As satisfaction levels get lower and lower customer supplier relationships become more tenuous, and customers looking for higher levels of satisfaction naturally migrate to other suppliers. The supplier becomes vulnerable to more and more competitors and as satisfaction levels drop still further, customer relationships can slide into the Zone of Customer Dissatisfaction.

The negative relationship.

When customers find themselves very dissatisfied with a supplier, losing business is not the only negative effect. As satisfaction levels drop below 4.0 customers go from disappointed to irritated to mad to actually becoming a dedicated enemy of the supplier. None of these things are good when negative word of mouth, public announcements of dissatisfaction, industry association complaints, lawsuits or even worse can result. All of these will hurt business and create a bad reputation that no supplier wants. These negative customer-supplier relationships open the door up to competitors because customers will choose – literally anyone else they can find rather than having to deal with the same supplier.

The Win-lose relationship

It's hard to call this a relationship, because the customer will run from this supplier after a single transaction. It is continually amazing how many suppliers operate routinely with a win-lose relationship model. Bait and switch, car repair rip offs, unjustified cell phone bills, irrational medical insurance rate increases, ridiculously high gas prices at the only station on the highway - there are too many examples.

Savvy customers know to stay away from suppliers like this but it's not always possible.

The supplier who can't or doesn't want to bother to compete with a commitment to excellence might decide to get what they can from single transactions, with no hope or plan for a future relationship of any kind. Although the win-lose relationship is unsustainable over time, short term gains by the supplier at the expense of the customer create animosity, and adversarial relationships between customers and suppliers develop for entire industries because of lack of trust that happens when customers repeatedly 'get the shaft'.

Anyone who has tried to book a hotel in Las Vegas during a busy time might experience a low promotional price, only to get there and be forced to wait in line for hours, have all kinds of extra resort fees, parking fees, taxes and other expenses tacked on – making the hotel at least or more expensive than some nicer ones – when you thought you were going to pay a low price. (See I just gave Las Vegas a bad rap because this happened to me recently – this is how it works).

Stuck with your supplier.

Win-lose relationships are especially frustrating when the customer has to deal with a single supplier that abuses the customer-supplier relationship by delivering poorly across the range of the Values of Excellence. Cell phone companies that surprise you with extra charges and penalize you for canceling your contract, local cable TV where you only have one choice of company in your neighborhood, or a health plan that doesn't let you schedule more than one appointment a month- these are all examples of suppliers who leverage these sole option/sole source positions.

Suppliers like these, who can avoid competing head to head with another supplier to keep a customer's business, are strategically in the position to consistently take advantage of the customer. Corrupt monopolistic practices force win-lose or no choice options on the customer. It's no surprise that customers don't like this because the chances of obtaining the excellence they want is virtually nil.

Free markets and competition create higher levels of excellence.

One of the healthiest things the American economy can do to help itself is to empower competition. When markets are truly fair and open, levels of excellence will increase because of competition, resulting in better choices for the customer. Suppliers have to continually evaluate their offerings to maintain customer satisfaction and loyalty and have their excellence shortfalls more evident when there is competition. Creating customer satisfaction means being competitive as a business. If you want to improve – perhaps the first place to look is to your competitors *to see what they are doing*. We recommend this for all employees.

Relationships take work.

As any marriage counselor will tell you, all relationships have their idiosyncrasies. Tolerating mistakes is easier if there are other admirable qualities there and the other in the relationship is doing their best to make an effort. Things seem to work out better when there is a sincere effort to maintain the customer-supplier relationship, and to do some things right that exceed expectations. Everyone appreciates this. Be willing to put in the work that great customer-supplier relationships take.

What you do as an employee or a supplier can have a big impact on the customer supplier relationship. This course is about being proactive about it.

II. How to Be Excellent

You will find nearly every aspect of the customer satisfaction experience represented in the following Ten Values of Excellence. It is helpful to think of brands or organizations you admire as being the best such as Rolex, Mercedes Benz, Apple, Ritz-Carlton, Gucci, Pebble Beach Golf Course etc. as you learn about each of these values. Inevitably, you will also be thinking of your own customer experiences where each of these values was present or lacking.

As you review each of the values of excellence and their definitions below, begin to think about how each will apply in your own situation at work or business.

Our in-depth statistical research into *what customers say they want* is summarized in these Ten Values of Excellence.

As you go through each of these values rate yourself and how you perform as an employee or the supplier in your relationships with your own customers. You can follow along with the Customer Satisfaction Delivery Self-Assessment included in the next chapter.

This is the meat of this course and what I want you to learn and to integrate as you relate to your customers. This course will help you create a fresh understanding of what customer satisfaction is really all about.

THE TEN VALUES OF EXCELLENCE
1. Quality
These are the factors related to quality that customers care most about.

Put yourself in the customer's shoes. Of course, customers want the quality of the products and services you buy to be delivered *right the first time*, with no mistakes, no errors and no inaccuracies. Customers expect the same thing. Getting exactly as ordered, no blemishes, the right count, the correct model, the latest version - all as promised, every time.

Designing product and service delivery so they are consistently accurate means a lot to the customer. Are you the type of supplier that commonly delivers with mistakes and expects the customer to 'take it in stride?' Are your processes and systems set up to check and double check what you do so you have the assurance to know that you are always delivering quality without defects?

Customers want the quality of the product or service delivered to be *consistent with the best available.* That means if you are serving steaks, customers are comparing yours with the best one the customer has ever had. Or perhaps you're not in charge of the menu or the kitchen, but as the server – you are responsible for giving the best service possible, as good as a customer might receive anywhere else. Whatever your job description or capacity as an employee, think about who does it the best in your entire industry, and compare what you do with them. How do you stack up? This concept of benchmarking- comparing yourself with the best, applies across every one of these values of excellence.

This is the way your customers are thinking – in the back of their mind they have an expectation of the best they have experienced or heard of somewhere else – this is always what you are being compared with when it comes to the concept of quality.

The customer expects everyone in the supplier's organization to *have general systems knowledge, know their own product line and be familiar with the latest developments and activities in the organization.*

Even though you may be the representative in your office who deals directly with the customer, the secretary or anyone else who answers the phone should also have an idea of 'what goes on around here'. Support personnel are a reflection of the quality of an organization and can make or break a customer relationship without anyone ever finding out about it. Knowing about the product line is another point.

How many times have you gone into a department store and the retail clerk couldn't tell you whether or not they had a particular item or where it might be? Asking where to find plumbing fixtures at the hardware store shouldn't require a consult with three different employees. Many of us can recall knowing more about an upcoming sale than the person in the store waiting on us. In actuality, everyone in the organization is on the quality team and should know their product line and what's going on. Excellent organizations understand this and understand that perceptions of quality are created by how well-trained their personnel appear.

2.

2. Value
The customer wants the best price that is available.

Each of us has a sense of fair play and no one likes to be taken advantage of. Shopping has become an art for some who enjoy chasing the lowest price. Many have personal Ego's that need to feel like their ability to negotiate or bargain will make a difference in the final price paid. No one likes to find out that the same item or service was available at a dramatically lower price somewhere else or even online, after they have made a purchasing decision.

As an employee, customers will appreciate it when you can put together offers, packages and inform them of opportunities to pay less when that is a potential option for them - especially when you really do offer the best price.

When you aren't in control of the price of the product, you need to be able to explain to customers why your price is justified compared with competitors or other options customers might have. Higher price but larger portions, higher price but comes with bonus features, higher price but all ingredients are organic and made fresh on site, higher price but the most recent version, higher price but is made in the USA, high priced bottle of wine but it was rated a 97 by wine spectator etc.

The customer wants the price paid to be historically appropriate with prices paid in the past.

Few things are more shocking to the customer than when a price jumps up significantly higher than what they are used to paying. The good prices might be one of the main reasons a customer patronizes your business, and when big price hikes happen, you may lose their business. Pricing is a careful strategy that takes many factors into consideration in everyone's business, and price increases are rarely in the employee's control.

So what can an employee do when they have to face customers with big price increases? The key here is to let customers know that their patronage is important to you and to provide some kind of reason why the price had to be increased. Depending on the situation you might be able to share additional information such as 'we are looking for a lower cost supplier' or 'we expect prices to go back down again when this crisis is over' or 'everyone in the industry has had to raise their prices because of the shortage of X' or 'our costs have increased dramatically' etc.

The key is to help dispel the impression that your business is out to gouge the customer, that you understand their reaction and value the customer-supplier relationship with them. While you may be providing damage control of sorts for uncomfortable price increases, you're also reaffirming the relationship with the customer to try and mitigate the negative impression. Customers appreciate it when they see a commitment to a relationship with them (more on this later).

On the other hand, if your prices have not increased over time, this is something you should emphasize at every opportunity with customers. Customers like to be reminded that they are continuing to make economical purchasing decisions

The customer wants the product or service to remain a good value over the long term.

Good buying decisions demonstrate themselves over time. Excellent products and services that have been designed with a long-term perspective become ubiquitous classics, and continue to act as brand emissaries year after year. Think of the old classic Mercedes, the dependable work horse printer, Craftsman hand tools with a lifetime guarantee, the local diner that has been serving customers for fifty years. Long term brand satisfaction leads to generational relationships with a supplier. "We have always been a Ford family" etc.

Additionally, your business might offer special warranties, a liberal return policy, discount coupons on your next purchase, member discount clubs, free oil change or similar value-oriented benefit to customers that will encourage an ongoing relationship with your business. Customers love these extras as they affirm their purchasing decisions and provide an extra benefit that increases the impression of getting a great value.

As an employee it is your job to emphasize the value to customers of having a long-term relationship with your business.

3. Timeliness
The customer wants the delivery of the product or service and all interactions with the supplier to be on time.

In this frenetic world, everyone has a lot to do. Being on time is a professional standard that communicates respect for the customer's time, and the fulfillment of an agreement to be at a specific place, at a specific time, to deliver the product or service at the time specified by or promised to the customer. Excellence means being early, or on time. Being late is not an excellent behavior, and not meeting critical customer deadlines has the potential to 'crash the plane' of any customer supplier relationship.

Timeliness, like the two previous values of excellence has a benchmark standard for being the fastest, having customers wait as little as possible and not wasting customers' time. When customers are made to wait longer than they believe is customary the customer-supplier relationship can be damaged. When customer expectations for timeliness are met or exceeded, the customer-supplier relationship will be improved.

The customer wants to take the minimum amount of time to get their needs met.

Excellent processes, systems, and interactions with customers are designed with minimum wait times, adequate staffing to handle multiple customers, and optimized transactions that take only as long as necessary. Each individual employee's actions can do a lot to create customer satisfaction when it comes to timeliness. Customers like it when they see you hustle to move faster so you can accommodate them.

Think about how much you yourself like to wait in line or wait on hold on the phone or wait for your food order to get to your table. You know how good it feels when the supplier is on time and how bad it feels when it takes the supplier too long. Great employees don't waste customer's time or make them wait too long.

The Customer wants the supplier to take all the time required to achieve satisfaction.

The flip side of the coin with timeliness is that there is a danger in going too fast. Shortchanging the customer by pushing him along too fast or not spending the time with them to fully understand and fulfill their needs can alienate the customer who might want a deeper interaction. Spending more time with customers is strongly related to the Value of Commitment (see below). As a busy employee its easy to look at serving a sheer number of customers, but the depth of interaction is another measure entirely.

When extra time is spent with customers it's an investment in the customer supplier relationship that can increase customer satisfaction.

4. Efficiency

The customer wants optimized processes which are as simple and linear as possible.

In these days of increased productivity there is no excuse for redundancy, non-linear processes, and inefficient systems design.

Wasting time and energy because you haven't thought of a better way to do things is a poor excuse. We've all been to a bureaucratic government office and been sent here and there, to come back for multiple appointments, only to find out that what you really needed was something else entirely etc. Customers want processes to make sense. The minimum number of steps, requiring the least amount of effort is the excellence ideal. Making things efficient for the customer means that customers won't give the supplier's processes and systems a low rating.

As an employee you aren't always in control of the process that's set up, but you have to use the systems and processes that are provided for you. Employees will often develop their own work-arounds in order to make sure customers get satisfied despite inefficient systems. As the ones with the experience on the front lines, employees should take a role in suggesting ongoing improvements to process and system efficiency to make things run smoother for the customer - and business owners should be listening to their employees.

Customers want a single point of contact.

Customers dislike telling their story many times to different account managers, or being passed from one department to the next with different representatives. When customers return again they want to pick it up where they left off with the representative they talked with previously, not someone else. They want to deal with one person, one time that is qualified to fulfill their requirements in a single interaction.

Employees need to understand that when they interact with a customer, these customers are putting their trust in them as the representative of the business in the customer-supplier relationship. Employees need to understand that in the customer's mind, they are the 'point person' with the customer's needs and requirements. Employees should understand this responsibility and treat the customer's faith in them with respect by spending the energy it takes and doing everything they can to make transactions smooth and efficient for the customer - before passing them to another employee or department.

5. Environment
The customer wants the supplier's environment to be clean, well-organized and aesthetically pleasing.

A well-organized environment provides assurance that the supplier has their act together. A disheveled, dirty, disorganized work environment immediately suggests a lack of confidence in the supplier.

Although standards of cleanliness vary widely from industry to industry-(the cleanliness and organization standard of a car mechanic is different than that of your dentist for instance), there is a benchmark for cleanliness in each industry and it seems a simple thing to observe the common standard for the business you are in- and then to set your sights on exceeding it to reflect excellence.

Excellence means implementing a high level of organization, cleanliness, and aesthetics. This is a tangible feeling one gets the first minute they enter a World Class business. The environment feels pleasing to the customer. As an employee it is essential to do your part to keep the environment customers see clean, well-organized and aesthetically pleasing – it's everyone's job and one of the easiest things to manage to meet customer expectations.

The customer wants to feel safe physically, in the supplier's environment.

Safety should never be an issue, but customers are regularly exposed to physical risks from exposure to coughing employees who should have stayed home, icy steps to enter the building, dangerous equipment they might be injured by, or even confrontations with unsavory characters at the corner bar.

Excellent Suppliers anticipate safety risks and clearly understand that an injury to a customer automatically turns them into a source of dissatisfaction and negative dialogue that will spread to many, potentially effecting a reputation for some time to come - not to mention potential liability exposure concerns. Customers appreciate you looking after their safety, and this is another way to demonstrate Commitment in the customer-supplier relationship (see below).

Psychological safety means making customers feel welcome, accepted and comfortable.

If you have been to a traditional Japanese Sushi restaurant, they often make a big deal about welcoming you and greeting you when you sit down at the Sushi counter. This makes customers feel immediately acknowledged and respected, emphasizes a willing serviceful attitude and lets the customer know that the staff are specifically there to serve their needs. Often, they make it a point to remember the customer's name - this is a great technique for any business. How many businesses could benefit from this approach?

Often it is the customer that must facilitate their own satisfaction by having to gingerly sweet talk or somehow manipulate an intimidating or irritating front line worker to get their needs met rather than experiencing an easy welcome feeling. Sour employees with a disdain for their own job or other negativity can give off a vibe that makes customers feel uncomfortable and tarnish an otherwise excellent experience. Some employees are just downright rude and mean. Customers should never be exposed to negative moods in the workplace from any of the supplier organization's personnel- especially when it creates an uncomfortable atmosphere or environment.

Employees need to do their part to make customers feel welcome and comfortable.

6. Connection – Ease of Access
The customer wants to be able to access the supplier's products and services easily.

Store or office location, hours of operation, and ease of parking are factors that need to be organized based on the customer's convenience. Even banks are recognizing the importance of this and are putting bank offices in supermarkets, opening on Sundays and have increased use of internet transactions 24/7. Great signage and directions to find the business can be another important factor.

Being accessible by customers means increasing use of the internet to be searched for and found. Websites, blogs, digital media such as video, RSS feeds, chat and other various online events can all be utilized to share information, teach, communicate and interact with customers to give them more of what they are looking for.

As an employee you won't always have control of all of these factors, however you can do your part in little ways to make sure customers can easily get what they need from your business. In a retail store, that might mean making sure employees don't take up valuable customer parking spots or that the doors are open on time. It might also mean staying open that extra few minutes when a customer walks in at the last minute – or making sure that all products and services are available until the last few minutes of the posted hours - rather than taking down early so employees can escape faster at the end of the day. It might mean taking the time to give exact directions over the phone, or walking the customer physically to the part of the store where the product is located so they can get what they are looking for.

In another business it might mean sending extra information links providing background information about a product or a service, driving out of your way to meet with a customer, or setting up a face book page to assist customers to get the information they are looking for. Think of all the ways possible to make your business easy to get to and find by customers.

Customers want you to be available, personally.

Answering your phone, or at least having a personal respectful message and getting back to customers quickly after they call is considered a professional best practice. Many are surprised at the number of CEO's today who actually answer their own phones and who recognize the importance of this as excellence in being accessible. Customers are duly impressed when you actually call them back - personally. Being available as many hours a day as possible- answering your phone and messages or being available to meet with customers personally is what customers say they want.

Connect with all cultures.

Excellent suppliers recognize the importance of including all groups and persons. Openness to connection is demonstrated by public statements to various groups, language translations, and accommodating various cultural preferences so they feel welcome and included. In today's diverse society, each niche represents a potential constituency that might mean more business. Inclusion as a business practice and strategy eliminates barriers to connection and increases the potential customer base.

No supplier wants to be known as an unfriendly provider to various groups or classes of customers. As an individual employee, your commitment to be inclusive of all cultures and types can be instrumental in increasing the size of a satisfied customer base.

7. Self-Management
The customer wants the supplier to be well mannered, courteous, and attentive as well as positive and enthusiastic.

Excellent front line service behaviors are one of the easiest areas of the customer experience to manage well and unfortunately, are often overlooked. The customer absolutely has no interest in hearing or seeing a bad mood, rude behavior, in being ignored, or talked down to. Suppliers who consistently bring unnecessary negativity or poor manners to interactions with customer will find themselves looking for new customers sooner than later.

Personnel who work solely on the phone must be extra careful to communicate warmth, receptivity, and respect as they are forming an impression, and indeed a relationship with customers – even without meeting them in person. In telephone situations, the voice and tone of the employee may be the most important part of the customer -supplier relationship.

As an employee – this falls into the category of what people typically call 'Customer Service', and is one of the biggest areas where you can have a positive effect with customers.

The customer wants the excellent supplier to have an appearance consistent with the highest expectations for the industry.

Dress, cleanliness, haircut, piercings and tattoos, shoes, makeup and more do make a difference and can potentially have an impact on customer impressions. Benchmark appearance standards, although they may be informal, are available in every industry.

Excellent suppliers strive to exceed the normal industry standard. Front line personnel are the supplier's emissaries, or in the case of the individual employee - how you appear is part of your personal brand image. First impressions of the entire organization start here.

Attitude of Service

An attitude of service doesn't mean that you are subjugating yourself or demeaning yourself in any way. Demonstrating a high level of consideration for your customers, anticipating their needs, and doing your best to fulfill their requirements is a fine art and is to be respected when done well. An attitude of service is always welcome in the customer supplier relationship. Bringing an attitude of superiority, entitlement, or other negative Ego manifestation is not what customers are looking for. If front line personnel cannot play this role in their job they should find another one.

Excellence means positively demonstrating great manners, a great appearance and the highest level of consideration and attitude of service for customers which is consistently positive and mood free.

8. Commitment To The Customer
The customer expects the excellent supplier to demonstrate that they have the customer's best interests in mind over the long term.

Commitment is the romance in the customer supplier relationship. The customer wants to feel like they are the most important customer and that they have your full attention. Demonstrating a commitment to the customer means continually soliciting their needs, making sure you understand them in detail and endeavoring to fill them. The excellent supplier is seen as working hard for the customer.

Maintaining a committed relationship with customers over time may mean staying in touch even when there is no business going on, and having other interactions that show consideration for them, their interests and their ongoing needs.

The Customer wants the Supplier to be honest and up front about all terms and conditions.

As any couple in a relationship will tell you, honesty is important. Suppliers who are caught being dishonest with customers have little hope of maintaining a long-term relationship. Providing all information up front provides assurances to the customer that there is trust in the relationship and relieves potential customer anxiety before it happens.

Excellence means that customers should never be surprised with expected outcomes that are not delivered or terms and conditions that were not discussed previously. As an employee what we're saying is that being up front with customers is always the best policy and potentially can have a big effect on customer satisfaction.

The customer wants the supplier to take responsibility when things go wrong.

In every customer supplier relationship, mistakes can happen. Customers want the supplier to inform them up front or as soon as possible when disappointments occur and to make amends when appropriate. Customers will appreciate the opportunity to change and adjust when they have up to date information -

even if it's bad news, and can minimize negative impacts if they get bad news in as timely a fashion as possible.

Making amends for an improperly prepared meal might mean giving it to the customer for free, or even adding a free desert if it means saving the customer relationship. Employees should have clear latitude with guidelines for 'making things right' with customers when mistakes are made.

Let's remember that we're talking about a customer-supplier relationship as a long-term phenomenon. Taking responsibility and making amends for mistakes in product/service delivery is a small cost for preserving a relationship that can be more profitable for the business over the life of the customer.

9. Teamwork
The customer wants consistent quality interactions with all of the supplier's departments and personnel and expects these departments and personnel to work well together to meet the customer's needs.

It is easy for those who are not on the front line with customers to disassociate themselves from the responsibility of a high level of service to the customer. It is not only important to emphasize a customer satisfaction-oriented culture in the workplace, but it is important for each employee to understand how what they do directly relates to the customer's experience.

When the janitor mopping the floor at the hospital was asked- "What do you do here?" he replied- "I am maintaining the highest standard of environmental cleanliness so World Class medicine can be practiced here. None of this can happen without me". Each employee needs to be able to trace what they do to the organizational mission of serving the customer and feel that they are on the customer satisfaction team.

Managing interdepartmental handoffs should be executed seamlessly, with personal introductions by the first employee to introduce the next representative to the customer when this is necessary - often with the original employee available for some time to support the new relationship if necessary. The customer wants to have the same great experience regardless of who they interact with in the organization, and wants to count on their needs being understood by everyone in the supplier's organization.

Customer Satisfaction is The Team's Responsibility

Excellent Teamwork also means sharing negative feedback from customers, even when it means bad news for another department or employee. If you know what's wrong you have a better chance of fixing it together. Teamwork means that a mistake in customer satisfaction is everyone's problem and everyone should be aware when it happens. This also helps support a team culture of self-reinforcement where mistakes with customers aren't often repeated.

Excellent Teamwork Is an Individual Responsibility

In the excellent organization, individual employees need to take inventory of their own teamwork behavior and honestly evaluate themselves and their own ability to work well with others - and to improve where they can. Each individual employee has the potential to bring synergy to the work group by adjusting and modifying their behavior to what will be most effective and productive to the collective effort and harmony with one another.

The Entire Supply Chain Is Part of the Customer Satisfaction Team

Vendors and suppliers should be made to understand and feel valued that they have been selected as a vital part of delivering satisfaction to the organization's customers. Developing these relationships with all parts of the supply chain has many benefits especially when the supplier needs special concessions, emergency shipping, or a sample in a different color to demonstrate excellent customer service.

Excellence means being great team players and promoting a teamwork culture with everyone inside the company as well as outside the company for the benefit of the customer.

10. Innovation
The customer wants the supplier to utilize up to date technology, processes and equipment consistent with the best available.

Excellence means meeting customer expectations by providing the latest, and the best practice for the industry, product or service. Excellent suppliers continually look for new approaches, new software, machines, processes, and knowledge to stay on the leading edge. Benchmarking outside of your industry is a good way to find new ways of doing things that others in your own industry haven't thought of yet.

The employee should embrace new improvements and innovations, software and systems when they are introduced – particularly in cases where it will have a direct positive effect on the customer experience.

Competition is Healthy

Competition can be the healthy stimulus that pushes the supplier to try new things, often leading to improvement. Excellent companies are more proactive about looking ahead and are not afraid to look to their competitors - even when they have a seemingly secure market position.

Excellence means advocating for innovation, and tirelessly looking for new solutions to old problems, and being the first to experiment with new methods. Excellence means fostering idea sharing and creativity and embracing new contributions from any quarter including looking at the competition. As an employee you can bring a lot to your own business by staying in touch with what competitors are doing and bringing these ideas up for consideration.

Making suggestions for improvement and innovation is a positive action for any employee.

Your Professional Development

Taking a proactive approach to your own development by learning more and developing yourself makes you a more important and valuable employee. If you are continually advancing yourself through education and training you will naturally bring new ideas and improvement to everything you are doing. This can result in real benefits passed on to customers and all of your customer relationships.

Everything we've listed here is measured in our Customer Satisfaction Delivery Self-Assessment to follow – where you can measure your own Customer Satisfaction Strengths and Weaknesses. You might want to take the Self-Assessment now.

III. CUSTOMER SATISFACTION PRACTICES – SELF ASSESSMENT

This is a confidential self-assessment of your customer satisfaction-oriented behaviors and practices at work, emphasizing each of the Ten Values of Excellence. It is completely confidential.

Be honest and objective with yourself and answer each of the questions on a scale of 1 (lowest) to 10 (highest). Add up and calculate your scores at the end of the assessment and read the analysis.

Everyone can identify areas where they can improve as well as identifying areas where you are already doing well when it comes to customer satisfaction.

This self-assessment is purely for your own benefit in targeting specific areas where you can become a stronger employee in the area of customer satisfaction practices. If you are using an e-reader to view this book- simply mark your answers on a separate piece of paper.

QUALITY

1. I always get it right/accurate/error-free the first time with customers.
   1 2 3 4 5 6 7 8 9 10

2. The product/service I deliver to customers is consistent with the best available anywhere.

1 2 3 4 5 6 7 8 9 10

3. I am very familiar with what my organization does, the entire product line, and the latest developments/activities (sales promotions etc.) and I can effectively share this information with customers.
1 2 3 4 5 6 7 8 9 10

VALUE

4. I can effectively represent product/service line price and value options with customers to support their buying decisions.
1 2 3 4 5 6 7 8 9 10

5. I can effectively respond to negative customer reactions to large price increases.
1 2 3 4 5 6 7 8 9 10

6. I can effectively represent to customers the value of a long-term relationship with the business.
1 2 3 4 5 6 7 8 9 10

TIMELINESS

7. I am consistently on time with customers.
1 2 3 4 5 6 7 8 9 10

8. I make it a priority have customers wait as little as possible for product/service delivery.
1 2 3 4 5 6 7 8 9 10

9. I take all the time necessary with customers to achieve customer satisfaction.
1 2 3 4 5 6 7 8 9 10

EFFICIENCY

10. I make every effort to deliver products/services to customers as efficiently as possible.
1 2 3 4 5 6 7 8 9 10

11. I am proactive about suggesting improvements in the business to make product/service delivery more efficient.
1 2 3 4 5 6 7 8 9 10

12. I understand that it is important for me to do everything I can for a customer to answer their needs before I pass them off to another employee or department.
1 2 3 4 5 6 7 8 9 10

ENVIRONMENT

13. I take responsibility for keeping the business environment my customers see clean, well-organized and aesthetically pleasing.
1 2 3 4 5 6 7 8 9 10

14. I make it clear to my/our customers when we are watching out for their safety.
1   2   3   4   5   6   7   8   9   10

15. I make sure my/our customers feel psychologically welcome and comfortable.
1   2   3   4   5   6   7   8   9   10

CONNECTION

16. I do everything I can to help customers more easily access our products/services.
1   2   3   4   5   6   7   8   9   10

17. I make myself personally available to customers as much as possible.
1   2   3   4   5   6   7   8   9   10

18. I am inclusive of all races, cultures and types in all my activities as an employee.
1   2   3   4   5   6   7   8   9   10

SELF MANAGEMENT

19. I am consistently well mannered, courteous, polite and enthusiastic with customers.
1   2   3   4   5   6   7   8   9   10

20. I maintain a professional appearance consistent with or exceeding the standard of appearance for my industry.
1   2   3   4   5   6   7   8   9   10

21. I consistently demonstrate an attitude of service with customers.
1   2   3   4   5   6   7   8   9   10

COMMITMENT

22. I consistently demonstrate my commitment to a long-term customer-supplier relationship with customers.
1   2   3   4   5   6   7   8   9   10

23. I am always honest and up front with customers about all transaction details and information.
1   2   3   4   5   6   7   8   9   10

24. I take responsibility and corrective action when things go wrong in product/service delivery with customers.
1   2   3   4   5   6   7   8   9   10

TEAMWORK

25. I work well with fellow employees to meet the needs of customers.
1   2   3   4   5   6   7   8   9   10

26. I am active in promoting a culture of teamwork with co-workers to improve the customer experience.

1 2 3 4 5 6 7 8 9 10

27. I promote teamwork at all levels of the company and with vendors and suppliers for the benefit of customers.
1 2 3 4 5 6 7 8 9 10

INNOVATION

28. I am open to learning new processes, techniques and technology to improve the customer experience.
1 2 3 4 5 6 7 8 9 10

29. I am active in suggesting innovations and improvements to existing processes and procedures.
1 2 3 4 5 6 7 8 9 10

30. I am proactive about learning and developing my expertise and professionalism in my employee role.
1 2 3 4 5 6 7 8 9 10

Add up all of the scores for the questions above and Divide By 30 _____
The result will be a score between 1 and 10

_____

Interpreting Your Score:

1.0 - 4.1 Damage Control

Things are not going well around you and you know why. You're not satisfying customers, in fact just the opposite. With these scores you might consider whether you are in the right trade. Scores in this range represent a lack of commitment, and a lack of focus on the customer relationship. This general neglect might be interpreted as actual adversity towards the customer. Get busy and start fixing things if you don't want to develop a negative reputation or
lose more business or support from the few customers you may have left.

4.2 - 6.2 Low Hanging Fruit

These scores represent malaise and mediocrity, and nothing special or memorable with customers. Just getting by and a maintaining are the descriptors here. Look in most directions and you can find things you can do to make improvement, a little bit or a lot. You may not be experiencing any sort of challenge or complaint from customers, but you are not providing much to admire either and therefore having little positive effect on customers or anyone else.

Although things are not necessarily bad, other employees with a stronger customer satisfaction focus are probably being welcomed by those around you.

6.3 - 7.8 Almost Good

You are on the right track as an employee focusing on customers, and good things are happening. Just on the border line there has yet to be created consistent positive return and recommend rates and loyalty effects as a result of your efforts but it won't take much to get you there. Attack a few of your lowest areas and build on a few of your strengths and you should see customer satisfaction levels and customer relationships improving. It may feel comfortable and manageable now but a little more effort will put you into actual positive territory with customers.

7.9 to 8.5 Satisfied

There will be evidence of your consistent practices, with positive feedback and returning customers. You may in fact, be the benchmark in one or two areas at your business and be creating very positive levels of customer satisfaction as well as building strong customer relationships. Don't get overconfident but you are doing well. Customers will recognize you when they return to the business.

Remember that you can still slide back to the previous zone if scores in just one or two areas drop unexpectedly. These are admirable scores and you will be the envy of most around you. It has taken work and commitment to get to this point, but an extra push in very strategic areas will get you even higher to the top. Keep up the good work!

8.6 to 10.00 World Class

You're a great customer satisfaction leader. The effects of what you do are known to many and you are considered a benchmark provider of your work, product, service, management or leadership. Your customers are extremely satisfied and are spontaneously recommending you to others. You are most likely sought out as an authority and expert and your name is synonymous with quality. You are leaving most of your competitors, if you can even call them that, in the dust. Congratulations. Your success is speaking for itself. You are an example for others.

Improvement Plan:

The three lowest scoring questions were:
Q#_____
　Q#_____
－
　Q#_____
－

These should be the areas to focus on first for improvement

　My top three highest scoring questions were:
　Q#_____
－
　Q#_____
－
　Q#_____
－

These are natural strengths for you that you can increase for an even more positive effect

IV. Listening to Your Customers

One of the biggest problems with many businesses when it comes to customer satisfaction is that there is no systematic measurement of customer satisfaction. In the first place, there is an incomplete understanding of the Ten Values of Excellence so the owner or manager of the business is not tuned into measuring the correct things or they might tend to misclassify the feedback they do hear from customers.

The second problem is that there is no truly systematic schedule or methodology for data collection from customers. Many businesses have what we call smiley sheets that might ask several general questions from customers, but even when they do get feedback the questions are too general to apply to anything specific, or they have terrible scales that don't reflect the detail necessary for customer behavior prediction (we use a 1 to 10 scale as mentioned previously).

Another problem, particularly with smaller businesses, is that the owner will either think they 'know it all', will make excuses for individual customer complaints, or will react very emotionally to one or two customer comments which are statistical outliers (rare results) that aren't really representative of the more general satisfaction trends they should be paying more attention to.

So how can you, as the employee help your enterprise get better customer data and try to identify things that might need to be fixed to increase customer satisfaction?

Here are a few tips that will make you an active member of the customer satisfaction improvement team, and might even get you noticed by the boss – or help you convince them to start a more consistent and methodical approach to collecting customer satisfaction data.

1) Begin listening to customers and writing things down. If you're an employee that deals with a lot of customers like a server in a restaurant for example – your simple questioning of your customers at the end of the transaction will give you some data to work with. You can ask leading questions such as: Is there anything about your customer experience we could improve? Or "This is your chance to give me any feedback about your

experience today – really you can tell me anything and I will write it down for feedback to our management".

Yes, you can always say "How was everything?' or "Did you find everything you were looking for today?" but in their rush to check out- as in the restaurant example, this type of question will seem more like a polite platitude than an honest inquiry about satisfaction and generally not get you the depth of information you are looking for and that the business can use to make improvement.

2) Keep a record. Let's suppose you are a server and wait on 40 tables in a shift. Out of the 40 tables you asked for feedback, ten of them gave you some actual information. Three comments were about slow service, four comments were about food quality, two comments were about not being able to park and one comment was about the noise level of the music.
As you collect information day after day, these same ratios of comment might be the same and tend to repeat themselves. You might get additional comments in other areas of course, but

the bottom line is you are keeping a record of the feedback that customers are complaining about – and which things keep coming up most often.

At the end of the week you won't just have a feeling about what customers might be feeling – you'll have a pretty good idea about those satisfaction issues that keep coming up.

Now when it's time to share this information with your boss or manager, who may or may not be expecting this, but you have the opportunity to present your data in a more reliable sounding format. Instead of saying "well customers are complaining about our slow service and the quality of our shrimp cocktails", you can say something like: I surveyed 2 hundred tables of customers this week and seven percent of them or 14 customers complained about slow service and 8% or 16 customers complained about our shrimp cocktails". Do you see how this sounds a bit more definitive?

At this point you might decide to increase everyone's attention on the subject, look for validation from the other wait staff or decide to do a more in-depth study of the particular issue of the shrimp cocktails.

3) Driving your satisfaction study deeper, you might want to collect data from the other wait staff on what time of day or which meal service where particular complaints seem to happen. You can also analyze particular groups of customers for their feedback – does the breakfast crowd feel the same as the happy hour crowd? This would be important information to know so your restaurant can adjust accordingly.

4) Once you have done a bit of this type of anecdotal data collection with rudimentary methods you might begin to build motivation for a more consistent data collection methodology. In the restaurant situation, a typical methodology is to include a pen and paper type card customers can fill out while you are processing their payment or towards the end of their meal. Use the ten Values of Excellence as a guide for the types of questions you should be asking.

In this situation a restaurant customer might not be motivated to complete a long series of questions but a few open-ended questions will allow you to examine the answers later to qualify and quantify what customers are actually saying. Questions like: What suggestions for improvement do you have? Do you have any comments related to the quality of our food? Is there anything else about our restaurant that you think we need to address?

These types of questions will draw a wide range of feedback, but the feedback will often give you much more specific information that the typical: 'How was your experience?' Rate your answer on a 1 to 4 scale.. blah blah. this type of question gives you nothing useable.

There are some problems with paper customer surveys once they are 'institutionalized' because in restaurants for example, after a while, the staff pretty much ignores them and don't present them to customers well, or managers cease reading them at all. The potential good thing about creating systems like this is that there is an ongoing consistent data collection system that can be continually analyzed. A well-designed system like this will allow you to change questions as needed when you are studying different aspects of satisfaction so you can target improvements.

Simple processes like this when shared with other employees can help develop a customer satisfaction focused culture and get issues out in the open so they can be agreed to and consensus can be developed about problems that might need to be addressed.

In the case of slow service for example, these discussions might be all the motivation needed for the kitchen staff to change some things about how they do things to solve slow service problems right away.

Other problems might be more complex and require more study – the important thing is to do all the research you can before decisions are made involving big changes that might cost time, energy and money until you are absolutely sure they need fixing. This data will help support your decisions on what improvements to the business are indicated.

These simple tips are hardly the whole story on customer satisfaction measurement, but they do represent some ways you can take a more active role in paying attention to customer satisfaction for the benefit of your business. Remember every business is on the customer satisfaction improvement journey – and you can help.

If you are interested in a more in-depth course about this subject and making serious improvements to your business as a whole we offer another course called:

<u>Guaranteed Success – The Secret Science of Compelling Your Customers to Return</u>

This is a 3.5 hours 18 video course with in depth organizational audit and improvement tools- great for any business owner or manager, but certainly a great professional development course for employees as well - check out more information here:

If you are interested in further study get my latest book:

[Becoming Excellent - Applying the Ten Values of Excellence To Your Organization](http://www.BartBerry.com)

Bart Allen Berry is an organizational development consultant and trainer who has provided employee and management training for more than 200,000 worldwide since 1985.

Bart is the author of many business development titles on Customer Satisfaction, Leadership and Teamwork.

Learn More at
http://www.BartBerry.com

Appendix:

44 EMPLOYEE TIPS FOR IMPROVING CUSTOMER SATISFACTION

1. See Customer Relationships as long term relationships with your business.

2. Start out new Customer Relationships right by making sure the environment is ready for them (clean organized etc.) you are efficient and on time, courteous, warm and welcoming and let them know you are here to serve them.

3. Introduce yourself where possible with customers – as early in the relationship as possible. It's still good to wear a name tag in retail situations etc. because customers will often forget your name quickly and it might make them uncomfortable – so make it easy to remember your name.

4. Think of how you are going to make it feel like a win-win relationship for the customer.

5. Tell customers you appreciate their business.

6. Plan and prepare to get it right the first time with your first transaction with every customer.

7. When you give your product or service to the customer check and re-affirm: "Is this what you wanted?" or "Is this the way you like it?" etc. This will let customers know that you have heard their needs and are catering to them and you are committed to the relationship y giving them what they need.

8. Ask the customer: "How does this compare with the best _____ you have ever had?" You will either learn that it is great, or the specific things that can be improved.

9. You can also ask them: "How does our business compare with the competition?" "How do we stack up?"

10. Ask customers where else they go and where they might shop, or what similar products they might buy.

11. Study Your Product/Services line in detail.

12. When employee training is provided – get everything you can out of it, but most importantly – get understanding of what the employer really wants you to be able to do.

13. Have a good idea of the types of specials, packages and especially money savings offers your business can put together for particular customer interests and share them with customers when appropriate.

14. When customers complain that prices have increase dramatically be prepared to justify these increases with specific reasons.

15. When prices have been held low for long periods of time be sure to remind customers of that as part of your commitment to the customer.

16. Know all of the aspects of your product/service delivery that support long term dependability of a product or reinforce a long-term customer-supplier relationship such as: Return policies, money back guarantees, repair policies, membership cards, volume discounts, customer loyalty offers, special sale events, free drinks on their birthday etc.

17. Try to be the fastest in delivery the product or service without sacrificing quality.

18. Compare how fast you deliver your product/service compared with competitors.

19. Remember to spend more in depth time with customers when they need it.

20. Try to do things in a smooth and efficient manner – when you have repeatable processes and systems continuously think about how you can make them more efficient to better serve the customer.

21. See yourself as the 'point person' in helping the customer get his needs met.

22. Do what you can in every instance to keep your work area that customers experience to be clean, organized and aesthetically pleasing. Don't think it's beyond your responsibility to take out the trash or lend a hand so customers don't get a bad impression.

23. Look out for the safety of your customers – icy steps, sick employees, construction work on site, slippery floors, dark parking lots, other misbehaving customers – you get the idea.

24. When customers arrive greet them warmly and make them feel welcome. If they are returning customers try to remember their names and let them know it is good to see them back.

25. Appreciate that your business has customers and treat every one of them like gold regardless of how tired you are, how close to closing time or whether or not you know a particular customer to be a pain.

26. Do everything you can to make information about your business/product/service as accessible as possible to customers.

27. Think of ways to go the extra mile with customers when sharing information about your product/service.

28. Make personal contact with customers with notes, emails, telephone wherever possible and let them know you are personally available for them when needed. Always have and share business cards.

29. Try to be inclusive of all cultures and persuasions when on the job as an employee – despite personal feelings or your own beliefs outside of work. Its business and everyone can be a customer and deserves to be treated well.

30. All those front-line customer service behaviors: Courtesy, enthusiasm, polite, warmth, cheerfulness – use them at all times.

31. Try to make sure to adjust your personal attitude and be in the right head space to serve customers at the start of every work day.

32. Take care of your work uniform, professional clothes etc. so your appearance reflects favorably on your business and meets or exceeds the standard of appearance for your industry.

33. Think of ways to actively demonstrate that you have the customers best interest in mind over the long term. Show that you are working hard for the customer.

34. Stay in touch with old customers if you can, regardless of how long it has been since they bought from you.

35. Make it a point to be very clear, up front, and honest about all terms and conditions of any transaction with customers. Misleading or lying to customers is something they are not likely to forget.

36. Take responsibility when things go wrong, when you make mistakes and do whatever you can to make amends

with customers. Remember you are trying to preserve the long-term customer relationship.

37. Make friends with your fellow employees and try to have great relationships to facilitate working better together and a positive work environment.

38. Become a champion of teamwork in your workplace.

39. Bring up discussion of regular drops in customer satisfaction/product/service delivery to everyone's attention in employee meetings and see what can be done to address them.

40. Do what you can to form positive relationships with vendors and suppliers so they will give your business better service.

41. Look at what other companies and the competition are doing that is new and innovative and think about applying it to your product/service delivery.

42. Be open to learning new technology and computer platforms that will make improvements to the customer experience.

43. Share your thoughts and insights about customer satisfaction with your boss or supervisor.

44. Develop yourself professionally, learn new skills, techniques and technologies to be more effective with customers.

© Bart Allen Berry 2018 All Rights Reserved
www.BartBerry.com

This book will also be available as
a short video course
at our website.

www.ingramcontent.com/pod-product-compliance
Lightning Source LLC
Chambersburg PA
CBHW030452220526
45464CB00006B/2502